FORCEPS

Poems about the Birth of the Self

Wendy Hoffman

KARNAC

First published in English 2016 by
Karnac Books Ltd
118 Finchley Road
London NW3 5HT

Copyright © 2016 Wendy Hoffman

The right of Wendy Hoffman to be identified as the author of this work has been asserted in accordance with §§ 77 and 78 of the Copyright Design and Patents Act 1988.

All rights reserved. No part of this publication may be reproduced, stored in a retrieval system, or transmitted, in any form or by any means, electronic, mechanical, photocopying, recording, or otherwise, without the prior written permission of the publisher.

British Library Cataloguing in Publication Data

A C.I.P. for this book is available from the British Library

ISBN-13: 978-1-78220-410-7

Typeset by Medlar Publishing Solutions Pvt Ltd, India

Printed in Great Britain by TJ International Ltd, Padstow, Cornwall

www.karnacbooks.com

FORCEPS

CONTENTS

INTRODUCTION ix

Forceps 1

Returning 2

Daniel 4

When Things Become People 5

Swimmers 7

Marital Suite 9

Birthday 13

Agency's Team Meeting 14

The Lake 16

99 Cents 18

Even When So Distant … 19

Megan and Rose 21

Old 23

Kugel 25

Trash	26
Dissociation	28
Mallomars	29
The Cashier	31
The Intelligence of Water	33
The Mauve Room	35
What Ballet Does	41
East Baltimore	42
Winter	44
Ode to a Persimmon	46
Desperation on the Drenched Schoolyard Track	47
Knitting	49
Family Dinner	51
My Mother Reading a Junk Romance	52
The City	53
The Apology	55
I Hold My Brain in My Hands	57
Dye	58
Silence	59
The Rash of Shame	61
The Voyeuse	63
To My Unknown Children	65
The Exile	66

Outlining the Floor Plan	68
Sooke	70
Birth-day	71
Old Dog	72
The Unconscious	73
Joy	74
Vacation	75
The Search	76
The End	78
Immortality	80
The Pursuit	82
NOTES	84
ACKNOWLEDGEMENTS	85
ABOUT THE AUTHOR	86

INTRODUCTION.

My life has been marred by the practitioners of advanced, criminal, secret mind control. I thought I was a normal girl from Queens, New York. For most of my life, I had no awareness that I was treated as a controlled specimen.

The search for my true past came in distinct waves. This collection of poems includes some from the long period when I knew something was drastically wrong but didn't consciously know what that was, and some from the breakthrough when I discovered my never-bloomed self. The poems cover the outskirts of my awakening, my plowing through and arrival in the middle of awareness.

The worst part of this kind of horrendous abuse is that controllers usurp a sense of self. The poems describe my fight to find what I had but didn't have, what slipped away in infancy, my early frost. Now I'm holding on; it won't be taken away again. I have regained a real, not imposed, self.

I never sit down to write a poem. A strong emotion or idea grabs and wrestles me down. That's my first draft. The poems come when I'm just waking up, walking my dog, grocery shopping, whenever. I often write on the backs of opened envelopes.

Once I realized my past, I wanted to communicate it. Poetry can make a narrative and thoughts oblique. The jumps that render poems compelling also distract and sometimes confuse the reader. Primarily, I wanted to be understood. When I started writing, I wrote poems about emotions, my family, relationships, food, and politics. But my mission of informing the world that this kind of abuse is happening today pushed me into prose. I wrote *The Enslaved Queen: A Memoir About Electricity and Mind Control*. A second memoir, *White Witch in a Black Robe: A True Story About Criminal Mind Control*, has also just been published. I had to be clear. These are exposé works.

Creativity saved me. When enforced, dissociated memories and emotions exploded inside, they eventually filtered into a poem. The horror transmuted itself. These poems are that record. I'm publishing this book not to expose but for the pleasure of writing.

People think it can take minutes to write a poem. There are long preludes to the appearance of poems. One brings one's whole life to the work. A poem that spits out in minutes may have decades backing it up.

FORCEPS

I swim down the Channel,
faster in a tempest

hold my arms forward and fit
through a hole

I can find you, you in the depths
among transparent weeds, ferns

I arch back hearing the sea shells,
my toes point shivering

the tide goes through my teeth
I remember you soft, thinking,

bold, mean
trembling, hidden, scared

fierce
yearning takes me into canals,

tunnels, subterranean paths
my heart's prongs grasp,

probe their way back to
the petrified of the lost *ago*

RETURNING

after Zagajewski

I walk on childhood sidewalks
past states, boroughs, counties
following invisible footpaths
and transparent voices
to the place where I was born.
Dew covers the cement.

The maple trees are decades
older. Their foliage falls leaf
by leaf
after the rains yesterday
came down in a frenzy of anger.
I used to pick up the samaras,
open them, stick them on my nose
pretending I was Pinocchio.
I pull from the trunks a strand
of aliveness.

The ash trees look grayer.
Gardens covered with weeds,
bushes with thorns,
thickets
of untrimmed joy flowers.

I see the corner of 108th Street
and 69th Avenue
and its mailbox.

My mother told my sister to mail
a card to a friend with cancer.
My sister's mittens were so thick,
she didn't feel the envelope slip away.
The friend would die
without having received it.
Cruelties hang in the air
unabsorbed.

My conscience feels scorched.
The hills—a mother, the breeze—
a lover, comfort.
I round a sharp corner, a courtyard
of secrets.
The flagstones screech.
I close my eyes and see blood.
Stones are older than the hatred
born here.
I scoop up a part
of myself and carry it away.

DANIEL

He said goodbye and turned. Circling, the swans shrieked.
He walked down the dark, narrow corridor.
He turned slowly to go. The swans in the falls screeched.

My eyes followed his tall, slender form praying.
His eyes held old philosophies and the future.
He said goodbye and turned. Circling, the swans shrieked.

Trembling light moved away from me blessing.
He waved his soft hand and the air's fibers tore.
He turned slowly to go. The swans in the falls screeched.

He said goodbye never to be seen again.
Be as pure as the swans, he said to me before.
He said goodbye and turned; circling, the swans shrieked.

His black curls whispered songs. The moon hummed above.
The elevator opened like a gaping furnace.
He turned slowly to go; the swans in the falls screeched.

His back moved away as his eyes watched me.
His young body glided through planets, leaving me on earth.
He said goodbye and turned; circling, the swans shrieked.
He turned slowly to go; the swans in the falls screeched.

WHEN THINGS BECOME PEOPLE

When you live without a mother or father or sister
or brother or son or daughter or cousin,
then the cherry blossom tree outside the living room
window becomes a harbor in April,
and the jalopy in your driveway
some okay man galloping to your rescue;
and the lavender on the neighboring hills
a person in the doorway singing welcome home.
The mango dripping has more
than a mysterious taste;
food becomes the older sister, a family
at the round dining table, close.
The chest with old mellow wood
your childhood friend.
The wing chair is the therapist
interested in your story.
The old flannel bathrobe with a few holes
and faded flowers that were too cheerful anyway
a refuge from disgrace,
the wool you knit
the weaving conversation at dusk.
The mattress is his embrace.
You make vows to the hot water bottle.

When you have lived alone for most of your life
and are aging fast, then the scruffy dog
is the toddler you raised forty years ago.
You still rush home, sniff, yell, and praise.
Your feet hear the earth beat,
the way your head rested on his heart,
before he left.

SWIMMERS

The chlorine-soaked air curls
to the faded white ceiling tiles and oozing grout

as the seniors in the free lanes kick
and the fast swimmers drive

in the left lanes of the Y at 66th Street.
The lifeguard levitates, scrutinizing

the crowd smothering the chemical water.
A whistle shoots each person, a siren

pierces the cement walls.
Each witness halts on edge,

the men tapping their feet,
locking their jaws.

The waters sink into a blanket,
the women shake under dark

purple towels like shrouds.
The medics unfold an old man's body.

In the water near the steps to the pool,
his heart imprints its silhouette.

The seniors shyly return to the stranger's grave,
dangling their legs at the shallow end

as the fast swimmers make up time,
circle lustily and hit

the under soles of the feet
of the body in front of them,

while steam hovers above the pool
like a climbing curse.

MARITAL SUITE

1: Myles at the mountaintop

We climbed a mountain with other students
galloping to the top where jubilant birds
somersaulted. I sat down at a distance.
Was this disobedience or how I really felt?

his eyebrows like reptiles' feet asked.
I also was surprised that I sat apart,
the hardness of my bones sending shoots
through the fossil-old rock that no-matter-what lasts.

2: Myles dining out

We were in Calgary so he could study.
He liked to eat in a restaurant every night.
His newspaper reached from one end of the table
to the other, rippling like a high tide of fights.

I stared at the tiny print on the front and read.
I could poke the page and hear him squawk but
that night I left. "I had to ask a waiter
where you were. You embarrassed me," he said.

3: Myles and money

"You'll have to support me during graduate school.
It's a good deal for you. Then you'll be supported
for the rest of your life. You're lucky," he said.
I thought of my grandfather leaving Galicia at fifteen

escaping conscription. He was short like me
and had a determined devious look.
He became a dress manufacturer in New York.
I felt my heart boiling into my ribs.

4: Myles and spaghetti sauce

A neighbor gave me her family recipe
for sauce with meat like anchors floating in ribbons.
It simmered for three and a half hours.
In my kitchen, you could climb the steps of spiced aromas

to ecstasy. Italian matriarchs
stuck their heads out of windows and smiled.
Myles opened a can of white clam sauce. I frowned.
The matriarchs swooned, later vulture-swooped down.

5: Myles and Vietnam

No, I was not ready to have children.
No, I didn't want a child now.
"But I won't be drafted if you do," Myles said.
"If he dies, it will be your fault," his mother said.

Guilt turned into a pyramid and I couldn't cope.
He put his finger in the middle of one of my ringlets.
It was our second tender moment
and the jungle greens became moist with hope.

6: Myles and therapy

I was in Dr. Wodnicki's office
when psychiatrists listened, not LCSW-Cs.
Dr. W had only one good arm.
I told him how one night while we were walking

Myles put his arm around me and squeezed a little
like good support hose. Dr. W
said that even in the worst of relationships,
there are every now and then some good moments.

7: Myles and parenthood

"I don't want another child," Myles said.
The war was over. He supposed he was home free.
I already had morning sickness and felt attached.
"It's me or the baby," Myles said.

Dr. W said a man has no right
to interfere with a biological process.
I thought of the baby, smaller than my hand,
a shooting star that would leap but not land.

8: Myles and the start of the girlfriends

I came home early and found him with a
philosophy student. I knew Amanda.
I could see how her red pubic hairs
peeked through her undies. Myles drove her home.

Hours passed. When he walked up the stairs,
I lunged and scratched his raw, fallow cheeks
leaving bloody tracks with pink shiny buds
blooming like a new Christmas cactus.

Summary 9: Myles and fame

With no tenure, he became a chairman.
"This is the first smart thing I've done in a long time,"
he said. His head nodded in time with his brain's
alarm clock. He married a blond student.

(No alimony for me.) After
seventeen years, he spread to national range.
He needed a theme: students should be studious.
He had copied my college papers.

Marriages fade into the skies as bulbs
of anger and his lies dissolve into ripe earth.

BIRTHDAY

Azaleas spit up jeweled nipples,
bleeding hearts rip spare earth,

camellia bushes shout scarlet yellow blood;
lopsided magnolias erupt magenta blue

as I sing to my humming garden after its winter,
a chord in myself plucks out of the underworld,

out of tangled colonies of bulbs, grasshoppers;
as a slow bloom gleaned from the wise soil

spirals under my feet, up my vertebrae,
as a deliberate dove juts through green avalanches.

AGENCY'S TEAM MEETING

She spoke out and the Administration squeezed
her like a juice orange
until her perky spirit
crusted into dry pulp.

Ashamed, she resigned.
At her last team meeting,
her fellow social workers sighed,
offered gifts and pretended

she wanted to recede into retirement
like digested food.
As they ate their party cake, an endearing elephant
stepped onto the team's table.

Everyone thought it was an hallucination
or a cliché. The handsome animal was adolescent
and fit perfectly on the agency's
conference table.

It lifted its right hoof and put it down
near the supervisor's plate at the head
of the imposing table. The supervisor,
who waves a too wide smile

and kills ants with her whole body weight
asked with her melodious voice that hid
a long history of confidentiality mistakes
if anyone had cases to discuss.

The aroma from the elephant comforted
the staff, some reaching out to stroke
its young wrinkled skin, gray
with blues and pink.

The social workers wanted the elephant
to sniff and curl its trunk
and carry them away to live among savages
who will kill them in a bloody, forthright way.

The fired employee asked where she should turn
in her badge and key, her voice cracking
and rippling into sacs of thick fluid.
Alarmed, the elephant stood on its front legs

tilting the table like a seesaw
and spilling all the plates into the
supervisor's lap inadvertently.
Then the animal balanced on its hind legs

and with its trunk placed the fired employee
on its back and galloped through
the walls, down the stairs, out
the main glass doors

to the outside air
and the scent
of chill freedom
and wild sirens shrieking.

THE LAKE

A butterfly expands black and white wings
until its tendons sigh
then cocoon around its core.

Four others rise at different heights
as if each had a pillar of
cascading dirt.

The black and white one is still
as my heart skips stones
across a waveless lake

that the inner green
of ferns
frame.

Swimmers splash into frigid water
emerge into amniotic air
become mermaids

as they glide sideways
undulate with water spirits
levitate to the other shore

sunnier but fecund
filled with empty spaces of
unrelenting calm

and pulse
a language of rhythms
the wild, hidden

layers of earth, sky
melting into the color of water
smelling of the cold sun.

99 CENTS

Mama, I am shopping in the Turkish fruit and vegetable market.
They are hard workers and look a little like me.
It is always crowded because juice oranges
are five for a dollar, honeydews and cantaloupes $1.69.
Your beloved mangoes and persimmons are 79 cents each
and the produce is fresh, fresh.
You don't have to dig to the bottom
for the good ones.
Remember how you shopped in the Bronx
and on Lexington Avenue.
One greengrocer said,
"Lady, I didn't know I had such good fruit."
Mama, I often think about whether I will
want to see you in the afterlife.
You still wouldn't think I'm good or pretty enough
and now I'm much older.
But today, I wish I could show you
the Chiquita
bananas at 29 cents a pound and
the cauliflowers, medium size but pearl white,
for 99 cents.
You would nod.

EVEN WHEN SO DISTANT ...

It's cherry blossom season in my neighborhood.
My dog and I walk back and forth
under birthing trees.

Deep in sidewalk cement is the back of a bug,
bee, wasp or perhaps a seventeen
year cycling cicada.

One half leg or a bit of wing reaches up out of its corpse
and concrete as if still holding onto life, as if
clenching for springtime air.

A pale rust strip that sometimes shows
depending on the weather and lighting and
how clean she is travels

down my dog Blossom's spine.
On another continent in a different century
her terrier ancestors were bright orange. Breeders,

who only wanted the chameleon Cairns,
killed the litter's blanched ones
but hunters couldn't distinguish rustic colored pups

from thrushes and fields and shot their own dogs.
Then breeders and hunters allowed the dazzling
white ones to sparkle against thickets and groves.

Cement cracks and releases prey
trees slough debris
our pasts bleed out into color
only that which has a use persists.

MEGAN AND ROSE

"Jack threw down my doll and we are protecting our babies,"
Rose says in front of the slammed door,
her cheekbones raised on her meaty face,
her thigh raised to shield.

"The bathroom is the only door that locks," Megan explains,
with her doll tucked under her arm like a spear,
her stance wide and secure like Goliath's,
jaw stiff as Hercules',
her translucent skin radiant.

Megan is diminutive even for an eight year old
with wheat field hair.
Rose is her best friend, a five year old
with sunnier hair.

They race into the playroom and sit together
on the same swivel chair saying "Ougeleyoou"
over and over, their heels picking up
and going down as they bounce their babies on their laps
and admire Jack, Rose's twin, juggling two balls for them.

Then Megan makes room in her toy stroller
for Rose's doll, and they go for a ride
along steep hills.
The dolls' eyes remain constant

even when they spring high
as if on a trapeze,
sometimes colliding on a bump.
The child-mothers sit the dolls up straight again
and give the trailing Jack a wary, warring look.

OLD

Wind swept off my shirt and youth
    when I wasn't looking.
A silhouette lies on the crusted ground
    browned and curled.
The new generation of machine-bonded
young run over it without noticing.

My hair and teeth sink to the enamel earth.
My breasts grow larger
to proclaim their uselessness.
Crows pluck away my red shoes.

A tapering tunnel of gray bricks
and leaking mortar faces me.
My soul cannot squeeze through.
I do a sharp twist,

my bones whip away from the wind
sipping scarlet and sienna.
My soul makes zigzag shifts, my ribs
spike as I spiral into sucked out air.

I pull out my hair dryer
and puff up my flat silhouette.
With fierce birds, we fly over darkened
clouds, swollen bones and red shoes.

KUGEL

I was in the kitchen cooking breakfast.
"This is my mother's recipe for kugel,"
I said pointing to the coral paper, fifty years old,
with blue ink forming little rivers,
its edges like Queen Anne's lace.

My mother wrote joyfully,
"Your Tante Brandel's (after whom you are named)
recipe for noodle pudding."
Tante Brandel or another aged aunt
must have dictated it to her.

I was surprised my son took the time to read
both sides of this remnant of a life,
as his almost four year old pulled on his leg,
then spun around herself.

The water part of his and my eyes touched,
and five generations knotted for an ancient flash
before sliding off to indifferent tasks.

TRASH

My pleasure is on Tuesday.
All week I collect papaya seeds, egg shells, meat
wrappers, fish bones.
I start out with a super-size black plastic bag that
I tuck in a kitchen drawer.
Not stylish or good housekeeping
but efficient for me.
I put the rind and stem of my pineapple in it,
which take up room.
And I clear out the fridge of old food.
Then I wash down parts of its shelves.
When the bag is one third full,
I transfer it to the outdoor pail and line
the inside garbage can with a small bag.
As they fill, I drop them in the big bag outside.
On Tuesday, I finally get to dump it.
There. It's done. It's done.
Something is begun and over.
No repercussions and lasting ill effects
to live with your whole life.
It is a finished story, not needing rewrites.

I collected, deposited, and threw away.
A big noisy truck came to my rescue.
A fantasy book ending to something real.
An accomplishment before the
middle of the week.

DISSOCIATION

I unzip my skin and look inside. I see a colony of ants, each with a purpose and a name tag on blue striped shirts. Nancy, Sally, Richard, Ellen, Michael, Connie-Sue, Anthony work together but don't know of one another's existence. I see them sitting around a long rectangular rustic table. They sit down, they get up, they sit down, they turn around. They are afraid. Every sound hurts. Every breath pains.

I unzip my skin and look inside. My skin catches on the zipper. I turn my arms inside out. I cannot believe. I didn't know. This is my skeleton, bones of fear holding me up, collapsing, buried, young, kept alive.

The ants march through a long dark tunnel. They wear a light on their headgear. No light shines in the underground. They plod ahead to perpetual sameness, to nowhere and no age. They hold jars of terror. I lift a lid, I close the lid, I lift the lid, they close the lid. My feet dig in.

I take an escalator to the top floor. It looks so normal up there, controlled, refined. I zip up my skin and go to a masked ball. How long can I pretend? I unpeel my sticky smile, push the round button and take the elevator down, lower.

MALLOMARS

Mother opens the blades of the scissors I am not allowed to touch and makes a slit. Her deft hands release the machine-folded wax paper, the curtain goes up and the aroma of chocolate, marshmallows, and graham crackers mixes like a spring bouquet. I am intoxicated before I have a bite. I want the touch as much as the taste, shiny top hats, French black berets. I squish the top with my little thumbs. A million cracks as in one of the slabs of sidewalk, where the bicycles get caught and where we fall. I pick each piece of chocolate off with my short nails, suck on it and swallow. I chew little bits along the edge of the crust, then scrape the bottom with the inside of my lower teeth. I bite straight through. Soft, then hard, now all together, soft and hard. Sugar, sugar, sugar. A cotton candy, circus-type sugar, graham cracker bottoms, an almost healthy kind of sugar, and chocolate. My lifelong friend. Dark chocolate. God's gift to women and even little girls. I take sips of the Walker Gordon milk she has delivered three times a week. Chunks of cream float on top like icebergs in the Atlantic. I swallow.

We have so many Mallomars in my house that my sister and I don't fight over them. In this long, slender box the color of sunflowers is enough love to go around.

One day, my mother spotted that I ate eight Mallomars in a sitting, in seconds really. I was fast. It must have been springtime, maybe around my birthday, with a gentle wind, birds chatting, and the fragrance of lilacs creeping through the brick walls. She grabbed the box away, folded it up and put it on the shelves above the ice box. She hadn't discovered me yet pushing a chair to the sink, climbing up, then hurling myself on top of the refrigerator and leaning back as I opened the doors to this sugar Eden.

THE CASHIER

I saw a woman past retirement age,
my age, at Thrifty Grocery Store this afternoon.

She stood on her swollen feet all day
checking out people's food.

The shopper in line in front of me bought
a vibrant bulb of pinkish garlic.

The cashier whose dyed blond hair was short and neat
picked the garlic up with the corner of the lady's bag

so that she didn't have to touch it.
The customer said she knew someone else with this allergy

who had stopped breathing upon contact.
The cashier who wore tidy earrings smiled stiffly

shifted the weight onto her other sore leg,
nodded her head "Yes" as she handed the customer change.

I stiffened with guilt that I too caused her effort.
At least I didn't buy fresh garlic.

As she scanned my ripe mangoes, I wondered
what had happened to her husband

and why her children didn't give her money
and how long she could last on her trembling thighs.

THE INTELLIGENCE OF WATER

blocked
no escape
trapped
plastic pipes
ancient hard roots
dirt walls
it scratches a route
a circular saw
to free itself
burrows
to the prim north
cocoons in the walloping west
lusts for the eerie east
downstream
bites the languid south
pinching dirt
torrents falling on it
the water plunges into a crack
stalks solidity
marries earth
rushing speed drives
through a path
rips its pipe

throbbing
narrow wider
its fast tongue
shivers fans
licks soggy air

THE MAUVE ROOM

I tumble out of my heart.
I stand with my feet on the sidewalk
looking up at me.
Who is that tree trunk person
with hollow eyes and a sucked out face?
I couldn't be the me I know.
Yesterday, I went to your front door.
Snakes blocked the passageway.
Fifty-seven is too young to die
a sudden death,
no goodbye, no expressed gratitude
sailing between us.
After death, privacy is stripped away
like the husk on corn stalks.
The truth shocks in the sun.
Two addictions: shopping and food.
Waste.
How will I get through today?
It's too cold to weed.
I can dust all my books one at a time.

On the day after you died,
friends came to my house and brought food.

We sat at the dining room table
and I tried to eat for their sake.
I walked into the living room
and saw a smoky form
going up the staircase.
Were you going to my computer room?
Were you making a repair?

Two days after you left, I dreamed of oak leaves
falling on undisturbed snow.
The leaves turned to blood and I knew that you,
an Episcopalian, were home safe
in your new world.

Three days after she died,
I dreamed of my oversized monitor.
It was running but then half the screen went black
with a white design in the middle.
The picture came back and then went
completely black.
Black. No words.
No design.
No symbols.
No click click of a cursor.
I awoke with the reality
that she had died.
I liked the shocked feeling better.

Months had passed since the bariatric surgery
and she had lost almost one hundred pounds.
We drove to her favorite store, Coldwater Creek.
It has an American Indian primitive feel.

She had a discount coupon.
She shopped.
She tried on.
She bought a pair of blue jeans.
"I never thought I'd be able to wear a size eighteen again," she said.
She looked like Columbus discovering America.
She bounced and her hair flowed in the new world.
We drove home, my dog on my lap.
I leaned back on her heated seat.
She petted the dog.
The dog licked her face.
She smiled.
The dog buried its face in her hip
and pressed in its skull.

Your cats are hiding. Your dog is
at the neighbor's, her new home.
Pretty soon your home will be cleaned
and scrubbed.
You would have liked it clean.

Last year, she painted all the walls
on the first floor of her house mauve.
Mauve is a slightly depressed color
but with gumption and laughter.
Mauve knows the joy in sadness.
Nothing stops mauve.
It gets up and goes even when
it's not well.
She put mauve on all the walls
in a trance of love.
Her walls hugged her guests

like a dog whisperer speaking to wounds.
If you had something difficult to talk about,
then you wanted to talk to her.
She didn't begrudge.

Two years ago, we were at the Sheep and Wool Festival.
Cows were lined up in the stalls.
You walked up to a particularly large one.
Its brown resigned eyes and yours met
and wove together like the finest silk threads.
Your hands petted its giant head.
The barn filled with animal noises and smells.
Your heart came out of your body
and touched the cow's heart.
Its heart met yours.
That was the heart that thirteen days ago stopped
with no goodbye.

People want to tell you news:
Rick is closing his practice.

Your dog just started eating again.

Blossom is sniffing around
looking frantically for you.

Sarah got a bonus at work.

Carole had twins,
a boy and a girl.

My heart is convex
with crags and cliffs.

It's getting close to the weekend.
I have to call her and make plans.
We're going to Aseateague.
I skip to the phone happily.
I freeze and melt like a wax witch.

Saturday, when I visited you on the last
weekend of your life,
the air moved slowly.
You sat especially still on your new leather sofa.
Words hung in the air.
Heaviness dragged.
A force was in the room like tiredness.
Space collapsed.
Why didn't I guess this was the end?
Why did I get up to walk my dog around the lake
instead of asking you if you were leaving?
Why didn't I demand that you get another work up?

We drove past horse farms
and the long white fences painted patiently.
You barely spoke and I began chattering
on the last Sunday of your life.
You were carving out space
and I was filling it.
Talk, talk, talk will make you stay.

The wind is growling outside.
It is insatiable.
It must be looking for you.
We are searching.

I saw a flash of red.
I looked at the bush growing
in the garden below the deck.
Camellias bloom in March.
The blue red scorched the cold air.
Color drenched bleakness.
The earth felt soft, responsive
like a friend's breath.
You for the first time appear
as someone from the past.
I feel you dropping layer
upon ozone layer
from my present
and future.
I see mauve streaked
with ash
smiling.

WHAT BALLET DOES

I am taking a ballet class.
I put on leotards and tights
and little white slippers
like another skin hiding disappointments and defeats.
I step into a studio
after seventeen years of abstinence.
Where did the body that used to dance and spin go?
I remember the steps.
I feel like the elderly CEO starting a second family
with the blond suntanned twenty-five-year-old wife.
I'm not done yet.

EAST BALTIMORE

The woman who died in the fire had asked her sisters to come and get her. One didn't have a car. The other wanted $20 to drive from Catonsville to East Baltimore.

The sister who died in the fire had said there was a rat in the house. She was afraid it would bite the baby. She was twenty-three. She asked her mother, "Can't I and the baby stay with you awhile? There's a rat." The mother had said no because there were drugs where she lived in the ghetto and she didn't want her daughter to be near the drugs.

The woman who had a baby who died in the fire paid $300 a month rent. She was kind and took in whoever needed a home. She took in men who lived in her basement. The men were smoking in the basement. The men panicked when they smelled the fire and forgot about her and the infant on the third floor.

The woman who took in men who caused the fire had gone to the window. The men who had been smoking in the basement told her to throw her baby. She went to the window twice. Her sister doesn't know whether she was thinking about throwing the baby or just looking at the men. The sisters had relatives who had jumped. Their legs had been smashed. One died.

The woman who died in the fire was burned all over. Her baby died but had no burn marks. The sister said Jesus had protected the baby from the flames.

It was on the news all week. The sister of the woman who died in the fire said the news begged for money but no one gave. She said that people don't want to send money to East Baltimore.

The sister who doesn't have a car feels her body turning into butter. Her leg and head are shaking. Her mind is running. Her mind is driving. Her sister could have taken the bus. She could have stolen $20. Her mother could have taken her in. The mother said no. If the sister still had a job, she would have had a car.

WINTER

My heart jolts me.
It's 3 a.m.
I look out the bedroom window.
A Christmas tree is in the road.
I am alone.
A dim hum passes through thin, damp air.
I get back into bed.
It's very cold.
Someone cut down the tree, in its glory, for money.
It stood among family for just one week.
No longer a star or angel on top.
Someone else stripped it.
Ornaments put away for a different tree.
Tossed.
Spikes still green and moist.
Branches turning upward.
Taken away from water.
Lying on its side, flat.
I can't remember what happened to my engagement and wedding rings.
I hope I sold them but maybe not.
Look how my fingers are thicker.
I was thirty-nine when he left for my best friend.

I thought they were just colleagues.
Lying on its side, cold.
I bring my knees to my forehead.
The tree can't even comfort itself and fold.
It's better alone.

ODE TO A PERSIMMON

Your color goes through me like the heat of fire
or a roaring sunset,
blinding jewels.
You fit heavy, soggy in my palm.
Your mouth molds around me like a bosom,
my flesh sealed to yours, dripping, pulp drenched.
Your sweetness will not turn on me or desert me
for more pristine lips.
You will slither down my throat
and coat my vulnerability with love.
Your taste quickens my blood rush.
As my eyelids close, I hum.

DESPERATION ON THE DRENCHED SCHOOLYARD TRACK

An old carpenter injured on the job
couldn't stand the spiking pain
from the barometric pressure of the wailing
wind that slashed the vinyl walls
of the neighborhood homes.
His frozen shoulder and dead right arm
reached a fever pitch of pain and he panicked
and shot out of his house to the schoolyard track
in the blistering rain. It was 4 a.m.
dark and hollow. His umbrella blew inside out.

The woman he sometimes saw jogging
had just eaten three Hershey candy bars
and also rushed to the track to walk off the delicious
calories. She used to weigh 400 pounds.
Her umbrella gone, they walked,
not side by side, but in comforting
proximity. "You can get only so wet,"
he called to her cheerfully. They sloshed
in the bubbling mud, even their underwear
hung heavy with ice rain.

They saw another man slouched under the downpour.
Worried, the panicking man got out his cell phone.
The dieting woman's hair stood up
as the squatting man wailed sharp sounds
and remained in his stooped position
like a rock sinking into the earth
as the hurricane circled around the two pioneers
and over his bowed head.

KNITTING

Rip ten rows.
Rip the slavery marriage.
Rip the inverted childhood.
Extricate phony friendships.
Take the tweezers and pluck pompous boyfriends, two iatrogenic hospitalizations.

One stitch goes awry, causing the pattern
to bite its lopsided entrails.
If I rip ten rows, I could start again.
If the forces of life paralyze free will into schizophrenic choices and the wool knots,
I could take the tweezers and pull apart the intractable.

No fingerprints, lumpy betrayals, freak bus accidents, no children from the wrong man.
No ethical sinkholes, prairies of digested skin.

The pregnant secretary glows in flaring fuchsia pink.
The wool is no longer virgin but just as good if a bit weary.
If not used for four decades, it will be just as good
if a bit stingy.

To live as if it never was
is why women from the beginning do handiwork,
rip and do again without a trace.

No men vacuuming women dry.
No ungrateful children sprouting knives.
Rip the separation agreements.
Rip the in-laws.
Rip twenty rows.
Rip divorce lawyers.
Rip dropped stitches.
Rip more rows.

FAMILY DINNER

In Mother's home, there were few cooked dinners.
Occasionally we ate a whole broiled chicken,
and a mashed potato and carrot mixture.
My sister looked down at the potatoes
on her plate and said, "They have the measles."

Something must have been bothering Mother
that night because she banished her favorite
child from the table for using a
metaphor, and a good one; Mother who had
herself just said, "The pickles aren't so tired."

Their similes and imaginations
buoyed me above burnt words and sharp aromas
to the ice blue and rose world of aesthetics,
whose milk I suckled, a pulp I held onto.

MY MOTHER READING
A JUNK ROMANCE

You propped yourself up in your twin bed
with three down pillows, your head against the wall.
It was late morning, almost noon, and we
were hungry. We could have gone into the kitchen
to get cornflakes and milk but we weren't
allowed to make noise until you were up.
You hadn't slept all night because you don't sleep
and were relaxing. The paperback you read
was covered in brown paper but we knew
that it was a trash novel. Your index finger
curled your red hair as the rake seduced the
young married and carried her away on horseback.
You smelled of lavender as you twirled faster
and faster and they had sex in the open
field of poppies. The top of your nightgown
opened as a stalk of bananas ripens.
"He married me to hide his lack,"
you cried. I, spying, vowed never to marry.
"That makes me feel like I've been a bad influence,"
you said. I felt myself fly through the cattycorner
bedroom windows into the air that smelled of
lilacs and berries. I flew higher, closer
and closer to the strawberry sun.

THE CITY

I return to be dunked and dangled
in dope drenched air.
Horns, engines hacking,

crushed voices,
cumin and chestnut smells
lift me.

I ramble to where I used to shop
on 14th Street and up
the Avenue of the Americas

to where my father's office was
for forty-four years
and following the octopus energies

float down towards Elizabeth Street
where in my youth,
on each street corner

I had shed shards
coated with exhaust
and clogged ambitions.

I remember the man who worked in packing
for thirty-one years, went home at 5 p.m.
to his two-room walk-up where he lived alone

and died at 5 a.m. on his faded sofa.
I pass the bent over old who couldn't find a way
out shuffling in their contagious strength—

a woman older than the wars, carrying a bag
of apples and oranges up a hill, stops
to ask where the subway is—

and the ones who own New York
crunched scarves and strolling fingers
all roll over my numbed skin.

A giddy freedom seizes
and I dissolve
into the asphalt cement.

THE APOLOGY

She secreted a sexual vibe.
Men glimpsed her voluptuous hair
hungry eyes right away
even though she was a pastor's wife.
She and her husband practiced all the positions
but he deserted her anyway
for other wives.
Men kept after her.
She preferred body builders.

Her son became a body builder.
His muscles were like globes of the world
with ravines and seas.
Her daughter, asexual.

The son bought back the family home,
its backyard bursting with pink magnolia trees,
and he and his sister lived in it.
Eventually, he ODed by accident.
At the funeral were many young men
with orgasming muscles.

On Easter, the mother clipped
branches of magnolias
went to the cemetery
and laid them on his grave.
The pristine petals
were like beacons
calling out to the heavens.
The branches, the length of her body,
lay heavy, clumsy, stuttering
like a breathless apology.

I HOLD MY BRAIN IN MY HANDS

Intelligence slips through my index and third fingers.
Pieces at the edges crumble apart like feta cheese,
then the southwest portion of abilities falls away,
Klumt.
I am not aware.
My wrists levitate.

A string attaches to each rhythm in my brain.
I have a committee—a philosopher, homemaker, witch, slave.
The committee holds the strings inside and out.
Tighten, loosen, tighten, shove.

I look down at my brain from above
still in my hands.

DYE

I put my electric blue silk suit
that should have been dry cleaned
in the washer by mistake.
My new French socks
were spared somehow.
My underwear no longer counts
all that much.
But my pale pink nightgown emerged
tie dyed.
It must have wrapped itself around
the drowning blue suit,
gulped its poison and
spared the community.
My nightgown is a hero.
I fold my laundry.
I put on my streaked periwinkle nightgown.
During my dreams, it covers
the lifts and plunges of my heart,
its collapses and restarts.
Two friends just died, one at eighty, the other, fifty-seven.
The older's heart stopped, the other died after a gastric bypass.
The overrun with color nightgown is a meadow I sleep in,
my companion in catastrophe.

SILENCE

Where I grew up in Forest Hills,
four large prewar apartment buildings
were on the corners like giant wings.
My sister stood on the balcony
looking down at the geese and swans splashing
in the tiered waterfalls. She held one of the turtles
we bought at the Five and Dime Store.
She held it by its shell, its four feet dangling,
moving as if it were crawling safely on the ground
but faster, faster doing air walking.
My sister and I shared a bedroom.
She had dark curly hair
and looked like our Hungarian father
but her skin was rosy white.
She looked American and modern,
which was what all the relatives strove for.
Our grandmother and aunt became blond
and mother a redhead.
My sister stood on the balcony
in her red and white checkered dress and threw
the 5 & 10 cents store turtle.
Her high cheekbones went higher.
The turtle didn't drown in the water.

It landed on the sidewalk.
Then my sister ran through the lobby
and around the building. I raced after her,
trying to keep up with her longer legs.
A gang of children followed.
The turtle was upside down, its little legs running.
The turtle, who loved its shell, was trying to run from it.
She flipped it with her patent leather toe
and ran it over with her doll carriage
that she had left parked underneath the bedroom window
where she and I slept.
I backed up and pressed my back into the brick wall.
I heard only a slim crack as
when my mother boiled eggs, took a knife
and opened the shell,
scooped out the insides, yellow and white.
We ate the eggs in our narrow kitchen
whose side windows overlooked the waterfalls.
A boy flung the turtle into the water.
The geese and swans gathered.
Sometimes the water spoke as it rushed downward
into silence.
Whatever happened will be washed away,
whatever happened will be gone.

THE RASH OF SHAME

An insect
pivots
underneath the
bleeding bone

clamors its burn
until it paints
a butterfly,
its shimmering wings

silver, purple
taped behind glass
glued to paper
fluttering to take off.

Maroon wings
shed the frame
fly through cheeks,
shoulder, stinging womb

shredding tissues,
joints

imprinting
bowels.

An undercoat of purple
pops up
as the insect burrows
for another itching

wave.

THE VOYEUSE

You rushed through the lobby
Saturday mornings with long
strides
in polished shoes
barely alighting on the cement
like a skipping stone in clear waters
a tallith wrapped around your shoulders.

Two boys snickered, another threw stones.
"Misfit," they sneered. "Dumb ass."
Your round face softened and your eyes
became a split honeydew
oozing sweetness and vitamins.

Later your sons cleaved to your thighs
as you spread your tallith around them.
Clouds floated over a gray
dim sky,
sparrows rushed into branches
and the geese below exalted their wings
in rhythm with your fringes.
Your torso bobbed up and down

like the birds diving into the choppy
waters pointed east.

It began to pour but through my glass
and your glass, I studied your sheen.
The waters parted and veined the gleaming air.

I saw a father and two boys my age.
I saw safe love.
I saw an apartment outside the one I lived in.
I learned there was another way.

TO MY UNKNOWN CHILDREN

I am your mother and you don't know me.
Birth pains, cut umbilical cord, more to endure.
I never held you, will never look at you closely.

Two half-Asian, half-Jewish girls who flee.
Straight dark hair, hurt eyes of wonder.
I am your mother and you don't know me.

The image froze into a paralyzed plea.
A grasping couple with stealing nails roared.
I never held you, will never look at you closely.

I stayed connected until you reached three.
I don't know what continent holds the door.
I am your mother and you don't know me.

You don't know my skin, I know your tangled wounds
that track into a webbed knot others tore.
I never held you, will never look at you closely.

My screaming blood in your young blood, angry.
You know my scent, I know your tears that implore.
I am you mother and you don't know me.
I never held you, will never look at you closely.

THE EXILE

Along crisp orderliness
I greet immensely polite citizens
of exquisite civility
who smile widely with perky teeth
but I miss chopped herring,
knishes and rough expressions.

In passing we have long talks
on smooth sidewalks
about their rescued dogs.
The beatific landscape must chisel
pleasant personalities.
My admiration spent

I move onto a rocky path up a proud cliff.
I twist and slip in mud
but make my way to its steep top.
The gouache sky, a designed curtain, suspends
a dark strip of gray above a lighter mist,
purplish blues encompassing the pink peak,
clouds as motionless

as the breath between held back words.
I discern the molded peninsula of high growths.
How are you feeling today?
I, a refugee, ask the foreign heavens of swift moods.
Like an octopus she wraps herself
around me and the ancient mountain.

I stop by every day to see my only friend,
a hugging opaque sky,
a fountain of blintzes, latkes, matzo balls.

OUTLINING THE FLOOR PLAN

My mind sleepwalks past the dreary walls
and square foyer that we use as a dining room
through the hall with raised wallpaper covering built-in closets

to our room where my sister has the bed closer
to the windows with starched organdy curtains.
My parents double locked the front door for the night.

Our father's slinking, slurping steps skid
through the space between our beds, shove into mine,
the younger, and he spills my softness.

I run my eyes against the bumps and crags of the walls,
come to the deep crevice of the corner blue and rest in its arms.
I hear Mother shuffle down the same dark hall,

perhaps to save me, I pray,
her nightgown and loose skin trailing like wings.
His hard stomach leading, he scurries away

like a rodent pursued by a terrier
as her long silk fingers tremble into fists
pounding on the dough of my inner ear,

her teeth shining through her lip with saliva.
My sister's screams rise and embroider the Victorian prints
of ladies in hoop skirts and samplers stitched by children

who lived one hundred years ago as he
returns to drag Mother away, my mind
going back down the hall, past the gray foyer,

into the kitchen that Mother painted yellow and green,
their bedroom where they now lay as if in a grave,
past the long windows of the living room where the family

watches shows of fathers being fired, mothers burning pots,
sisters arguing over sweaters, past the elongated bathroom
with black and white scrubbed tiles

back to the double locked front door for the night.
As I wait, my mind whirls around itself outlining their paths,
searching for escapes, policing the terrain.

SOOKE

islets of blue sand float
over ancient pre-storm seas

my new friend with a lace-
edged frayed soul and I

kidnap sorrowful wind-washed stones
which press into our soaked palms

as if looking for our inside beat
will they be lonely away from their siblings

silver cumulus clouds breathe as our feet
dip into raw granules

soon the violet tide will storm
as we return to our ordinary

BIRTH-DAY

On a forest path studded with hypnotic bouquets of wild red, yellow, and purple emerging from a green carpet of shiny, pointed leaves, I feel a kiss slide and press in, though it is not physical. It coats my face and tells me I am someone's child.

I cannot tell whether this voice comes from my desperate inside warriors or the pregnant outside. As I thread over soft earth and ancient stone, a healthy umbilical cord descends from beyond a spotless sun through choppy clouds on azure.

It is spring and my birthday. The air smells of swollen summer.

After seventy tortuous, orphaned years, a pleasure joins to my barren lips.

I walk in a light jacket along a squeezed path and belong.

OLD DOG

I forget to bring the driving directions
and know right away that means
I don't want to go.
Then I feel your muscles tugging,
your eyes needing,
your underwater current pull me.
It reaches through reservoirs and lakes,
pipes and drains, beneath hedges
and lawns and up
the backs of my legs.
My nerves explode,
their filaments stretch over airways
and mountains, weave around clouds.
I rush to pack as I think of your
getting older and withered.
Any time may be the last.
My heart grows large.
I step through its silk door.

THE UNCONSCIOUS

Asleep, I hear
"Put a few tablespoons of strong tea
in your strudel dough and it won't be dry."
I perch with the wild geese on the high
lighthouse
in the stormy, roaring Pacific
then fly to Belarus looking
for this great-grandmother baker.

Quivering, I roll over to my right side
as my dead childhood friend presses his heart.
Our beats form the same music.
He flies through the tangled ceiling
as I roll onto my stomach, my feet paddling.

When I wake up,
I stand,
wash my body cool,
iron my blue striped shirt.
My fashion shoes clunk.
I chew perky protein and crunchy carbohydrates.

Glazed, I sit until it is time to sleep.

JOY

Alone and dying
I reach out my hand

expecting to touch
a purplish thorned

knuckle

instead I meet a velvet
sateen.

My shocked heart
spikes

to the camellia burst

the magnolia palm

the ancestral fingers
of the half moon.

VACATION

I want to be home
below the crust of the air, in bed.

Leaving for two weeks is like trekking
on cracking ice

diving to the polar earth for one fish
polishing the periphery of stars

instead of being tucked in
with my imitation down pillow

automatic shut off heating pad
and wide sea of books

as my white dog nestles at my curled feet
as the alarm system embraces my walled dreams.

THE SEARCH

I am looking for my sister outside
a Broadway theater.
It's a surprise.
She doesn't know I'm waiting.
A fast sunset strikes
the soot streaked façade's entrance.
The audience floods out the main
and side doors.
There's a woman with long dark hair.
It's not her.
There's a fur coat. Wrong person.
I see a green scarf. No.
I am eight years old again with
no one to play with.
I latch on to my older sister
as the only one who might understand.
I follow her from room to room in the apartment.
Spectators jam the stage door.
They stream out thickly.
So many faces.
I search and search and
sink into a haunted hopelessness.
The crowd dissipates.

Trains with corpses
sift through the dark
as families search and search
at stations, as tracks disappear
into the hollow night.

THE END

In Forest Hills, where I grew up,
sewers were at each street corner.
I never saw them overflow
into the gutter.
Once on a dare, I stuffed
a boy's jacket through the iron rails.
His mother found out and peered
in the sewer. She saw it
floating in the water
its arms stretched out in grime
but didn't tell my mother.
I had done something wrong
and then there was grace.

At the end of love,
the air goes counterclockwise,
birds land on higher trees,
and my heart, like an accordion
with one part cracked,
closes and opens,
a bent over heavy blossom
on a fragile stalk.

When love is gone,
after the explosion,
I unfold my body,
gather myself from the floating grime,
bring in my suspended arms.
Threads and streams pour gravity
back into my creased vertebrae
and piece me together.

IMMORTALITY

Runners weave through her ovaries,
her daughter's and her daughter's daughters'
until their daughters' return to the earth
where they will be rolled out like rice dough,
strong and viscous, into bouncy, sticky kernels.

Leah is steaming prune dumplings for Mother's Day,
scooping them with a slotted spoon when her daughter
returns from a cousin's wedding,
leans over to gather daffodils under the kitchen window,
her balletic spine elongating like her mother's.

She and her fiancé foxtrot up the petaled front steps,
through Leah's moist kitchen, onto the deck's laden balustrade
slowly tangoing under the crescent pine trees and vines.

They dip into the underworld, her hair brushing the glazed rock,
then breathe in the white skies
as they arch under an open rainbow.

In Leah's traveling sleep that night,
she straddles a plump swan whose penis
points to heaven and breasts drip vanilla malteds,
flies over pollinated meadows
disseminating figs and pecans

that smaller birds will carry off for their own young
as generations of Leah's kin trample the fecund fields
bringing home wildflowers and fallen grains.

THE PURSUIT

Once a day, a servant, perhaps a mother,
leaves dried bread crusts and water
at the threshold.
Once a month, an orange.
I bring them apples that I have
stuffed in my apron pockets
and open the cavern with a universal key
that I have caught from the clouds.
It is shaped like a fish and opens doors
no one can see. With MacIntosh
apples in our mouths, we crawl
on our stomachs through jagged tunnels
that former prisoners dug,
go deeper into
the earth,

walk along the foundation
where rodents scurry and sniff
and arrive at the side basement door
that creaks from disuse.
I emerge into daylight
on the other side of the building,
into a strange yellow light, untouchable

and air that tastes sweet and bitter
like an overripe mango.
Juice drips down
my throat as I think
it was worth it.

NOTES

"When Things Become People," was published in *Passager*, 43, Winter 2007, and *Burning Bright, Passager Celebrates 21 Years*, 2011, both edited by M. Azrael & K. Kolpelke. Baltimore, MD: Passager Books.

In an earlier form, "Kugel," was published in *Mudfish*, 15. New York: Box Turtle Press, 2007.

"Dissociation" was published in the online *Survivorship Journal*, 21(1), Winter 2016.

"Birthday," was published in *Welter*. Baltimore, MD: University of Baltimore Press, 2012.

"What Ballet Does" and an earlier version of "99 Cents" were published in *Mudfish*, 16. New York: Box Turtle Press, 2009. "99 Cents" was nominated for the *Pushcart Prize*.

An earlier version of "The Voyeuse" was published online at *Network of Spiritual Progressives*.

"Birth-day" was published in *Passager*, 2015.

ACKNOWLEDGEMENTS

My special thanks and appreciation go to Baron Wormser, Judith Harris, Elizabeth Kirschner, Jill Hoffman, and Mary Azrael.

ABOUT THE AUTHOR

Wendy Hoffman is a survivor of organized criminal abuse and has been a psychotherapist for over two decades, working in general practice and the field of recovering dissociated memories. She has a Master of Social Work and two Masters of Fine Arts. Her first memoir, *The Enslaved Queen*, was published by Karnac Books in 2014, and a second volume, *White Witch in a Black Robe*, followed in 2015. Now that she has brought together the separated parts of her mind, taken her life back, and achieved freedom, she wants to help other survivors also become free of mind control.